The Phoenix Living Poets

———— ⦻⦻⦻⦻⦻ ————

AIR AND CHILL EARTH

Poets Published in
The Phoenix Living Poets Series

★

JAMES AITCHISON

ALEXANDER BAIRD · ALAN BOLD

R. H. BOWDEN · FREDERICK BROADIE

GEORGE MACKAY BROWN

HAYDEN CARRUTH · JOHN COTTON

JENNIFER COUROUCLI

GLORIA EVANS DAVIES

PATRIC DICKINSON

TOM EARLEY · D. J. ENRIGHT

JOHN FULLER · DAVID GILL

PETER GRUFFYDD

J. C. HALL · MOLLY HOLDEN

JOHN HORDER · P. J. KAVANAGH

RICHARD KELL · LAURIE LEE

LAURENCE LERNER

CHRISTOPHER LEVENSON

EDWARD LOWBURY · NORMAN MACCAIG

JAMES MERRILL · RUTH MILLER

LESLIE NORRIS · ROBERT PACK

ARNOLD RATTENBURY

ADRIENNE RICH · JON SILKIN

JON STALLWORTHY

GILLIAN STONEHAM

EDWARD STOREY · TERENCE TILLER

SYDNEY TREMAYNE

LOTTE ZURNDORFER

AIR AND
CHILL EARTH

by

MOLLY HOLDEN

CHATTO AND WINDUS

THE HOGARTH PRESS

1971

Published by
Chatto & Windus Ltd
42 William IV Street
London W.C.2
*
Clarke, Irwin & Co. Ltd
Toronto

60703

ISBN 0 7011 1831 8

© Molly Holden 1964, 1971

Printed in Great Britain by
Lewis (Reprints) Ltd, Tonbridge

For Alan

Acknowledgments

Acknowledgments are made to the editors of the following journals for permission to reprint poems previously published by them: *The Review* for 'The Gap', 'Suburbia, Like Hanging'; *A Review of English Literature* for 'Race Memory'; *The Times Literary Supplement* for 'Button Oak to Arley'; *Wider Horizons* for 'Putting The Lights On'; *Outposts Publications* for 'Hill in Winter', 'Childbirth', 'Illness', 'Winter Quarters', 'Farm', 'The Dying Publican', 'Farm Boys', 'Memory Without Experience', 'South', 'Piper's Hill', from *The Bright Cloud* (1964).

Acknowledgments are also made to the Arts Council of Great Britain for financial assistance, 1969–1970.

CONTENTS

Illness

Poetic justice is imperfectly exemplified in me
who, as a child, as a girl, was persuaded that
I felt as earth feels, the furrows in my flesh,

buttercups curdling from my shoulder blades,
was what I saw. The rain would fall as pertinent on me
as on the lichens on the flint-embedded wall.

I had always a skin too few, identified
with sun-hot blossom on the far side of the road,
felt beneath my own warm envelope of flesh

the foreign winter that calcined the delicate
bones of the organ-grinder's shuddering monkey.
A ploughed field poniarded my chest.

So now it seems a wry desert that youthful
ecstasies, my earthly husks of joy,
should be so turned about by this disease

that feels like mist upon my fingers, like
a cold wind for ever against my body, and
air and chill earth eternally about my bones.

Hill In Winter

Briar and tussocked slope, unbeautiful
on November days with the small rain tangled
between twig and grass, have not yet lost
the year's last rags, brown straw not yet
completely sodden, the final leaves unmulched;
but the heights are almost stripped where
the wind always blows and on Liddington
nothing's left—the grass naked, a wet green
without nourishment, the thyme withdrawn, the turds
of sheep and rabbit hard, grey, unfertilizing.
Still it makes sense, the winter hill undecorated,
under the flat sky that casts no shadows.
Without it the fields would jumble, the hedges stray,
and the fork in the road lead nowhere of importance.

The Fields For Miles

The fields were misted with the cold for miles;
a devilish frost outlined hedge and roof
and dwindling stack, sharp as white acid,
not the showier and somehow reassuring ruff
of snow. I travelled that morning through
the southern shires by train, along embankments
and on levels where I saw the land laid out,
and what I most remember about
that winter is not that it was hard
and cruel after war but that, one morning,
from a shabby train, and cold, I saw
along the line and in unseen, remembered counties,
the trees all over England blossoming with frost.

Winter Quarters

The house that no one else would rent stood
oblique to the road, up a rutted lane
on a downland ridge, facing east; but the gipsies would
and now their carts and ponies in the rain
filled the black garden, shafts up-thrown,
rumps to the wind. Inside were damp floors,
rotting wainscots, a scullery of filthy stone,
windows without glass, rooms without doors.

This was for hibernation only, no need
to make for comfort; a roof to keep out snow
was all they wanted. This was as snug indeed
to them as any sett to badger, and would do
until the furrows softened with spring thaw
and they could move again, slowly going
about the sour edges of other men's law
and lives, watching their setting and sowing.

The Dying Publican

Panegyrics filled the small square bar that night
(he'd lain a week upstairs without a word):
"He'll not pull round from this," they said, "at ninety-
    two.
And yet do you remember how he skipped
between the tables still last week, could sign
a cheque with lovely flourishes, liked everything
just so?" Behind the bar, in tattered coat,
Bob drew the handles down, still helping out
the man he'd known from babyhood. "The last one
left," he said, "who's knowed him since he came."
Nobody minded the old tale that night, the mood
was on them all. "A wonderful man,"
he said, "they wouldn't touch the licence
while he lived but when he goes, you mark my words,
they'll be along with bulldozers and cranes,
and level the ground and make car parks on the stables
and strip these rooms and cart away the chairs.
Gin and Jags it'll be then and they little lights
in corners. There'll be benches outside for
the likes of us." The talk subsided for a while
beneath the blueness of the smoke; on the walls they saw
the things they'd always seen, brown photographs
of football teams of 1910, forgotten racehorses,
the pub itself so long ago the skirts of girls outside
in frozen attitudes did not show their legs,
and, in the corners, blackened chairs without
grace or antiquity. Upstairs there ebbed away
the life of more than a man.

Farm Boys

They are usually no more enlivening
than town boys with their muddy hair,
hobbledehoys lounging at the windy corners
of the Corn Exchange, guffawing by the doors
of village pubs, fooling on lanky bikes.

There is little to choose between them. No romance
enhaloes those who will grow, without luck,
to inherit the tenancy of a damp cottage
or, taking their fortunes in their hands, get
digs near Austin's and make more money at the bench.

We no longer credit the noble savage,
think all men drab; nevertheless, once,
setting out early on a summer dawn, the sun
rising into my dazzled eyes, I met a boy
driving a tractor-load of hay down from the hills,

singing above the engine's roar, his hair
top-bleached to saffron by the harvest sun;
so perhaps, in his triumph, might Vercingetorix
have stood, the golden Gaul, before the world
closed round him with its sober Roman fate.

Memory Without Experience

Riding back to lodgings in Salisbury one summer night,
his brain clouded with the day's memories of
heat, stones, earthworks, my grandfather
was knocked from his bike by a white owl
swooping from the dusk; so he came to his senses
in the downland grass, in a twilight without lamps,
one wheel of his overturned cycle still casually
free-wheeling itself at his side. He was a man
of little humour but laughed at himself in this,
wondered at the attack, and cycled on to rooms
where fire, meal, bed and breakfast cost five bob.

I did not even hear this from himself, it was
a secondhand experience when it came to me;
curiously I had no difficulty in seeing that
particular dusk, the sudden white shadow, and the
overturned bicycle with its slow-circling wheel.
I am not sure now that it was not myself who fell
into sweet grass in green twilight,
who remembers distinctly the bruise on the left knee.

South

Since sailing finished these must be
the loneliest seas in the world—Cape Horn,
Deception Island, the whole uninterrupted sweep
of latitude fifty south. Except for the odd
whaler or weather-ship, albatrosses only
frequent their surface; nothing hinders
the roll and collision of several oceans.
Unseen now, do they still exist? The men are dead
who sailed them but would have confirmed
their reality who held their ships
into the gale for weeks to round the Horn,
who burnt their hands on rope, who were
stunned by wet sails, who lay in misery in
swilling cabins to reach apricot continents.

Seaman, 1941

This was not to be expected.

Waves, wind, and tide brought him again
to Barra. Clinging to driftwood many hours
the night before, he had not recognised
the current far off-shore his own nor
known he drifted home. He gave up, anyway,
some time before the smell of land reached out
or dawn outlined the morning gulls.

                      They found him
on the white sand southward of the ness,
not long enough in the sea to be
disfigured, cheek sideways as in sleep,
old men who had fished with his father
and grandfather and knew him at once,
before they even turned him on his back, by the set
of the dead shoulders, and were shocked.

This was not to be expected.

His mother, with hot eyes, preparing the parlour
for his corpse, would have preferred, she thought,
to have been told by telegram rather
than so to know that convoy, ship, and son
had only been a hundred miles north-west
of home when the torpedoes struck.
She could have gone on thinking that
he'd had no chance; but to die offshore,
in Hebridean tides, as if he'd stayed
a fisherman for life and never gone to war
was not to be expected.

The Same Bush, In Bud

Like old gold buried long beneath the earth,
coated with verdigris and cool damp mud
above a darkly sullen gleam of worth
— wink enough to the wise — so this bush in bud

glows with the smothered light of what's to come
exampled by a few voluted flowers
already out, like prints of some damp thumb
that liquefy the grime of chthonic powers.

I wait its revelation with grave glee
as the last cleaning of rich objects found
in Wessex tombs or Bronze Age sanctuary.
No casuistry needed here — the ground

has not been robbed of sacrificial goods
that men intended for their dead's delight.
This golden bush was meant to break the clods
of my rough garden and dazzle living sight.

View From Archdeacon Fisher's Library, July 1829, by John Constable

This is more than a sketch but was never
worked up for the Academy so that it glitters
with the exact amount of white light on the leaves
that's there in truth at four o'clock in the afternoon
but is not always credited by those who look
at pictures but not at trees. He's praised
for his skies and I yield to no one in my admiration
of those clouds, building along the winds; but
until I came to watch trees with such care myself
I hadn't seen how fully he'd set down
their presences, their characters. Here,
in this sunlit meadow seen from a north window,
only a grazing horse in occupation, stand quite clearly
chestnuts at the left with their solid blocks
of leaves, an English elm in dark festoons,
an ash in the middle of the field, all
movement and sparkle. They are probably
all felled now, but he's preserved them.

                        He also preserved
with his paint, at another time, trees on a slope,
standing as if arrested on a downhill walk
because they liked the place or were
no longer thirsty for the valley stream; and only he
has ever caught the spotlit theatricality
of sunset striking up behind September branches.

Reminders

The only gulls I see now are inland
in winter, flocks that sensed the gales to come
and let the autumn's west winds carry them
to fields and reservoirs whose every strand
provides more food than does the splintering coast.
I watch them glide and tilt, their angled wings
catching the sun; their winter silence hangs
above me too. O tides and sounds I've lost!

Poets had used sea-imagery and lore
long before they learned that, in pre-human time,
man had crawled out, prone and handless, from its slime.
These are familiar themes — sea-blink and roar;
so my precedent's an exiled Saxon's words
speaking of storms and splendour of white birds.

Childbirth

The broken clock in the cupboard
said ten past six all night and all night
I remembered Lawrence's line about women in labour
crying like owls.

        Did I cry so?
lamplight on high ceiling, waking and
enduring and falling to fragmented sleep
again, with these I spent eight hours
of solitary night. This is why women remember
childbirth. Darkness and pain are companions
not easily forgotten though the thin crying
of new company may come with the grey day
and occupy the attention for many years.

Car Poems

i

I feel the weight of the gate
the man pushes wide for his tractor
as we pass; I feel (who never sit
in sunlight now) the burning sun on my neck
that burns the neck of the boy
bending over his bike at the side of the lane.
The brushing against bushes, the shape
and shadows of barns, the broken stone
on the garden path, the draught
under the door — in one half-hour,
passing the spinney, the farm, the cottage,
I feel them all, one lifetime's
and another's lifetime's experience.
An abominable ability but one
I cannot help. It is so long since last
I felt a lane, track, grass, beneath my feet
you'd think the memory'd be gone —
but still (and strangely stronger as the years
go maddeningly by) it curiously persists;
and all the other things I watch men do
I feel, I feel, I remember.

How much more comfortable to accept,
to be content to sit and watch
the passing show, be uninvolved:
also how much more placid and convenient
for those who have to cope
with my occasional despair.

ii

I sit sometimes in an apparent stupor
in the car, letting it carry me, knowing neither

north from south nor east from west,
but seeing (more sharply than you'd think) all
the full trees of an English summer, the ferns,
the shadowy gardens of snapdragons and
lavender, glimpses of dung-starred yards
and the cowman and his dog knocking off
for the night; also all gates set
obliquely in hedges, the sudden definition
between the edge of the field and the edge
of the wood, the woodlark on the wires.

Unfortunately, a certain blur of circumstance
intervenes at times between me and them
— well, I cannot help but be aware
of immobility, and distance from the grass —
and only clears when I am home again.
Then, though, memory, sitting quiet, is
more immediate than the moment was
and that I could not share their air
is quite irrelevant; memory makes me watch
the world from my old stance,
as tall and sensitive as other men.

Sanctuary

This was the old strip where the railway ran.
Now, between motorway and new estates,
it is quite derelict. The unpatched road
leads only to a farm. Buildings and gates
have been destroyed. Wire boundaries the track
which now is grass, rails gone and signals down.
No children come, have better things to do
in the planned playgrounds of the tall new town.

Goat-willow, elder, gone—wild plum, and thorn
prosper along the platforms, crowd the shed.
This is a rich new waste for them to claim.
Birds have increased. Shy warblers shout at dawn;
goldfinches hang on every thistle head;
and butterflies and fireweed tower like flame.

Putting The Lights On

Now the evenings shorten.
   Still I gaze
into the subtly-coloured garden
   at ends of days,

at last dusk's rosiness,
   at shadowed grass,
until the children put the lights on
   and in the glass

I only see reflected
   books, white paint, chairs,
the lanky limbs and laughing faces,
   my tall sweet heirs.

Farm

Milking always seemed to have finished when
we passed; the trackway was broken and patted,
the churns on the rough table on the verge,
but no sign of cows or cowmen, heavy breath
from the sheds, clink of chain or bucket;
or the haywagon had just left on its way
down the fields behind the fir plantation
towards Liddington. Yesterday's wisps strewed
the path but the wagon was gone and its presumed
driver and men with hayforks in the blue dawn.
We always missed movement, came too late
or too early, seemed to miss every motion of life
that informed that farm for it always looked empty.
The mysterious inhabitants left signs however
that they had been there, half-open windows from which
they had just leant, mucky boots in the porch
they had but now pulled off, the fresh ruts under
the gate that showed they had pulled it to with a jerk
only the moment before we had arrived. That
we never saw them seemed more than a trick of time.

Warblers

There are, I think,
no creatures less like stones
than these who fling
their fine and tiny bones

about my land
with bright-visioned swiftness,
hunting ephemera
with sharp, stabbing deftness.

I wonder that
the race is not yet dead.
For all they're shy
they have no healthy dread

of cats, nor men.

As good as say Amen.

A Parish On The Wash

I libel it, no doubt; but odd dark thoughts
intruded on my mind when I first saw
that lonely land, the isolated farms,
the saltings out of reach of civic law.

The church was beautiful, set gorgeously
with flints as black as glass, but stood too tall
above the village, seemed remote from men,
as if it had no truck with sin at all.

Deserted lanes, wide views, the crawling tide,
looked sinister beneath the brightest sun.
Nothing definable, of course, and yet
it seemed a land where murders had been done.

At The Turn To Mere

In a year's time, or even less,
no one will know the smithy
once stood here, the cottage adjoining
on the right, both doors always open,
either to watch the traffic and the passers-by
or just because they were friendly people,
the old man and his wife. They died
last year; the cottage and its industry
had been tottering for years before.

Some things, though, will signify
its past existence for some time to come.
Nettles always crowd old living-space;
and in the garden grew and grows
an apple tree that will take years
reverting to small green crabs or quince.
Great fruit glows there this month
although the smithy door is down,
the kitchen's desolation.

Surely Only A Fancy

A tree like a flame in the hedge.

Crack Willow. Nothing else, save pear, has bark
so deeply fissured and pear's more regular,
its cracks in latitude and longitude, lozenges,
rectangles, plateaux of outer rind rooted in pith.
But this most flaunting of the willows twists
as it grows. Its bark seems laid in swathes,
in foot-long feathers curling at their tips.
The only comparisons that come to mind for this
extravagance are those of men's artifacts —
the convention for fur in Saxon illuminations,
Leonardo's quilled and swirled descriptions of water,
the patterned joints of jousting armour, and
folk-tale memories of feathered cloaks the heroine
unwrapped from a walnut shell, the hero used
for his escape. I have seen nothing as wild
as this before, on the tree by the ford.

                              I assure myself
it's curious and beautiful but immaterial.
It only serves to hold my attention closer
whose attention is now obsessed with every tree
because they also do not move — the elms'
January roaring, the beeches like pewter marble
in their groves. I feel a sense of company
(not always comfortable, I assure you)
and of identity. And this tree more than others
draws me in — I stare at it, my back
to the ford where the children splash and call
in the sunlight, and find myself watching
flaked water, figures, riparian willows behind me
as if through fraternal and observant foliage.

Astonishment makes me turn. And then I feel
the carved and writhing tree observing calmly
my cold shoulders, my resistant spine.

Suburbia, Like Hanging

Suburbia, like hanging, concentrates
the mind most wonderfully, points here a view,
a slice of sky, a pattern of quiet roofs,
the observation of a sunset hue

that's moved across a wall as soon as seen,
the marks of rain's long action upon bricks.
Well, praise it for this excellent effect
it has on men — though these are city tricks.

Delight's always available to those
who need no burning-glass to urge the fire
of empathy; yet I still count my luck
for this suburban view of trees and spire

that faces afternoon and evening light,
is limited by lamp-posts, fences, lengthy wires,
but might be heart-of-Wiltshire scenery,
the smoke from chimneys autumn's last field-fires.

Pear Tree And Pattern

This was the way round it was.
I saw the pear tree first, in March,
one of an ancient row straddling
a hill. Pear tree twigs are short
and numerous, thick-budded before
bursting, pointilliste in appearance.
Then the new-ploughed field caught
my attention, each clod with its
attendant shadow, and the tussocks
taller by the hedge and also
stippling the ground between with
thicker presences. Whether I then made
comparison with an abiding interest
in early art or later on
I do not remember but it was near
that time, suddenly seeing in
sword hilts granulated with gold,
in clustered dots of ornament around
scarlet initials of manuscripts, round flat
wash representations of earth-bound
saints, thus elevating them,
the clotting of spring blossoms, the
dappling of the soil that infuses
delight and airiness into the world.

They had fresher eyes then and
more desperate winters, the men
who patterned thus. Spring brought
savour to a tasteless world; they must
have noticed this increasing texture
in the trees and on the ground.
Also, these patterns belong particularly
to the temperate countries
where spring's like that.

It Is Not Bred In Me

It is not bred in me to overlook
the close at hand, the particular.
I turn my head to gaze at every meadow,
to stare through every gate that's left ajar;

am always ravished by a width of view
but see the harebell at the bottom edge,
notice the thorn that gives the panorama scale,
brown roots, white garlic, beneath the tallest hedge.

It's just as well these are my inclinations,
to cry: Stop here — or here, that I may stare,
now that I have no choice but to travel slowly
or watch the seasons stroll from dark to fair.

For now I'm set in soul as well as tissue
and doubly urgent longing fills my days
to put down surely what is my obsession
— the small cold characters of plants, each phase

of sunlight on the grass, colour of thickets,
the shapes of leaves, the self-sufficiency of birds
— urgent because so relevant, their life's as strong
as ours and will outlast me and my words.

c

Venus

Venus, this morning, shone
like a small fierce moon in the east
two hours before the sun.
I, awake and watching, saw
her climb or seem to climb
into the blue that would be the blue
of full day soon, diminish,
disappear.
           Of what use is this
observation? If I am honest, none —
save that it comforts me in affliction
and in more peaceful moments
makes me exult that
planet, tides, rain, sunlight,
westerly gales, pursue their courses
quite ignorant of me, and men,
and even of their own existence.

Ambivalence

This compassion contradicts itself, wishes to see
the abandoned cottage restored to dignity
of a dwelling, the atmosphere of use — a clothes line
stretched from outhouse roof to apple tree
on which the tea towels stir, the peg-bag weighs,
wood stacked by the kitchen door, mud paths
packed satiny by tread — yet would not lose
the overgrown corner by the spilling water-butt,
the thrusting meadow grass beneath the sagging fence,
or nettles that follow every human desertion,
raising tender standards of victory over the places
where men once dug or urinated or stored tools
and now do so no more.
                         Also, to rip away the ivy
is to remove the last sweet autumn meal, the final
flowers of the season, to under-privilege late bees,
wood ants, bluebottles, destroy the shadowed
hibernation of small tortoiseshells and the promise
of berried harvest for the birds in bitter months.

A Compensation

The day lasts longer in suburban gardens.

This pleasant contradiction is worth noticing,
some recompense for living on a bus route,
some comfort on return from country drives,
mourning the rosy grass, the tabby-shadowed vistas,
thinking all beauty's only where one cannot live.

For suddenly, see, from the window, bricks
that glow like roses, white paint that sunset
renders apparently immaculate again,
the glowing stone. These dead things give back light,
absorbing none, throwing it again into
the narrowest of gardens, giant-walled,
and when those too can hold no more (losing it
among the recesses of leaves and twigs and grass
as the fields do), still tall and glimmering
themselves, still redolent of day.

                              Inhabitants
of cottages I envied as we passed, looking on
Clee or Severn Vale or long home pastures,
are sooner in the dark than I, their small-windowed
living rooms twilit half-an-hour earlier,
their oaks soon brown as leather, meadows darker
than water, and the final frenzies wasting in the west
for lack of sighting-boards to catch last light.

A Metaphysical Afternoon

This room has several well-placed windows;
    when the sun shines, it shines in here.
And winter sun, low and intrusive,
    casts shadows numerous, known, and clear.

Recognisable twigs and chimneys
    show on the long white wall at noon;
these are reflected in the window
    that faces them across the room.

Reflected light, faint smoke, and branches,
    among reflected books and wall,
confuse my dreaming observation,
    through them, of sunlight's actual sprawl.

So I look through reflections of shadows
    to solids and shadows outside.
There, too, the darkness slowly lengthens.
    Shadows, shadows only, abide.

In That Particular Bush

The north-west wind in that
particular bush divides it on the left,
folds it back upon itself, then
drops, and all the leaves
flow back again and settle
as they were until the next gust
opens it once more and the cool breath
enters.

                The motion is exciting.
If one could think so chill a thing
as wind were sexual, then this is so
and legends of miraculous conceptions
on girls who fell asleep upon
Aegean beaches, neglecting to
cross their legs when Zephyr blew,
seem almost credible, in context.

The devil's too, was cold, they used to say.

Roof Over Their Heads

Late bumbles seek our westward facing wall,
warm still from the day, as sunset comes;
they boom at the cracks of windows, fling
cobweb from their crisp wings impatiently,
seek crannies where this late spring's north wind
has not yet needled out the heat, and fold
their long furred legs in the crooks of upper hinges.

We are a zoo. The more I watch the more
I realise this house accommodates not just
a man, a woman, two long children, and a cat,
but also peabugs, sparrows, unfortunately
spiders, hibernating butterflies, as well as bees,
bluetits under the ridge tiles, martins under
the eaves.   Whose ecology's predominant?

Peasant Stock

I would sit by the fire at night when
the children were small, too tired to go to bed,
elbows on my knees, chin on my fists,
leaning towards the warmth,

                and, sitting so,
felt myself melt into an archetypal
attitude — that of many women over
many centuries, shawled, in black,
crouching by the last of the day's fire,
their bodies still, their hands uneasy,
exhausted to the bone but a child's cry
would bring them up.

                Peasants bred me
as they did most of the human race.

Reflecting Gold

For a week or so in April these bushes
create light, flourishing deeper-than-daffodil gold
to the very tips of their twigs
and blazing in the dusk as if
departed sunlight shone upon them still.

This early beauty, though, is a trap of sorts.

Returning warblers, innocent from Africa
(are there no cats to give them warning
in winter quarters there?), dive into
these gold depths, no other cover being yet
available, but more for the ephemeral insects
seething there than to protect themselves.
Small, sweet, stupid birds, they slip
from branch to blossomed branch like
drops of moorland water and stir
the twigs with delicate energy whose
constant quiver catches the orange cat's
attention in the otherwise naked garden.
His disposition's slow but now
he's quick enough to catch those unsuspecting
atoms tripping down the trunks. He
presents himself beneath the yellow sprays,
a pearled-green body limp between his jaws,
the thrown-back throat of cream reflecting gold.

Along The Salt Way

An odd sense of old privacies returns
with spring to cottage gardens; now the crowd
of ancient plants and bushes is defined
by green again and blossom, like a cloud

flushed rose and cream, obscures the boundary fence
— quite stark for months, darkened by winter rain —
and the gaze is deliciously misled
to think that all beyond is garden gain.

Now paths lead secretly round growing plots
and none can tell what's at the garden's end
and roofs of sheds are softened by the trails
of bryony that hide the need to mend.

Now jasmine flatters the blank door and makes
small windows smaller still, but what of that?
Spring's sweet confusion of both leaves and light
creates a kingdom out of ten yards flat.

Browner Than Mouse

Branches apparently wild as a child's
thick hair, blown all whither-ways by wind,
this bush is browner than mouse but will be gold
with clotted buds within the month.

                              One instinct
makes me wish to reach and comb it with my fingers
as I would align the tangled strands
of my own child's dark mop; another's
jubilant with pleasure that this waywardness,
this apparently random growth, is
natural proportion, governed by supplies
of food, room, light, and is quite
                              untameable.

My Debt To Farmers

I prate of trees and meadows but am
no countrywoman. I have nothing
in common with farmers save perhaps
a liking for plenty of room and a knowledge
of seasons as they turn the farming year.
I am hardly even envious as I see them
stand and talk in atmospheric yards.
Some I hate, those who deny
sun to their hens, space to their hedges,
full life to life; and even those whose men
and boys on bikes and burr-eared dogs
still drive their cattle comfortably on
golden evenings on warm roads, for whom
we stop and wait delightedly, would not
care for my appreciation of their beasts'
taking their time to milking, their
uninhibited bowels, their melancholy.

But I am more than grateful to farmers.
The raw material of their livelihood
is also mine, valuable for different
and various reasons — fine grass, for hay,
the soil-conserving trees, the field of wheat
ripe-full as any harbour with the tide — profit
for them and properties for me. Even more
I like, though, what they curse, the places where
men's organisation has not quite succeeded
or even been defied, where the nettled wild
creeps back at the corner of a barn
or lichens viridify the gatepost's ridge.

So what's marginal land to them, rank corners,
unwelcome poppies, is for me the haunt
of a sharp-scented spirit which persists

in such tall edges of fields, in standing pools
among alders, and which provides me with
the solid food of a curious poetry.

Metamorphosis

The cottage people left the place
in early spring, shutting the windows tight,
taking the curtains down, all save
those above the sink, tissue-paper-thin
from years of steam — and also left
an apron, long-unused, hanging
like a ghost behind the kitchen door.
The woman took some plants, those
she had most loved, just showing green.
No sense, she said, to leave the roots
of phlox, forget-me-not, lad's love,
to be ground in by bulldozers.

But the demolition men were laggardly.
March became April, April May.
The sunlight strengthened, green thin shoots
began to palisade the path
with their frail shadowings.
Within the house, in musty rooms,
the warmth brought out some
hibernating flies and, from the folds
of that abandoned apron, one
small tortoiseshell who'd packed
her infant wings in that unlikely place
in colder months.
                    Later that afternoon
chance, or a stray draught in the shuttered house,
took her to the centre of the room
and light beyond the door
lured her to the equally airless parlour.
And there she stayed, fumbling
the small dull panes and resting
occasionally on the dusty shelf below,
already spotted with the excrement of flies
similarly immured, and harbouring

their concluding corpses. Cobweb
blurred the fine brown chequer of her wings
as she was trapped and struggled free
time and again from corners
of the spidered embrasure.

                     When, in June,
the first bulldozers breached
the walls, the long-staled atmosphere
exhaled, and breath
of scented summer was drawn in
too late. Dried abdomen
and folded drained-of-colour wings
lay tidily upon the window-sill.

Nadir

End-of-June blackbird and blue tit came
to the garden today, shabbied by fatherhood
—white sideburns streaked, black coat
unpreened and broken — silent now too
because the courting's over. I sympathised
with them, knowing that fledgeling shouts left
little time for niceties of toilet.

                Yet I imagined,
although I knew it wasn't so, that I saw
in them some remnants of that horrified surprise
the movement in the nest had given them
who had no intention of creation,
shock at the squirming life where there had been
only the soothing eggs to ease the nesting itch.

Their round eyes stared, they seemed still dumbfounded.

The Gap

There is a certain moment every
cloudless evening when the sun in summer's
level with the ground, its central rays
laid along grass and garden, piercing
the hawthorn hedge, the straggling peas,
the spinney, thinning out their shadows
and casting other shadows far afield
— the heads of elm trees, chimney pots.

To face that level blaze is to be
goldenly included, more than we ever are
at any other time of day or year,
in that bright gap of being between
the brilliant phlox and brilliant
crowns of beeches, an intermediate thing
that's not so colourful, with not so long a shadow,
choosing the place however, identifying.

ᴅ

Sapling Lime

Two years in the lawn and at last
it begins to look like a tree. Broom-head,
the children called it, lovingly mocking,
that first spring.

                    Now I am learning its ways,
its family traits, its family likenesses.
Like all limes (but I had not thought
so young), it has a tendency to throw out leaves
haphazard up its trunk; also I realise,
watching this slim thing grow, why limes
give such abundant shade — its bright
and rough-edged leaves are set
in circular canopies that overlap
by lobe and margin, impenetrably lush.

Its winter form's as much a revelation
as its spring identity; its twigs
grow with a certain double curve
that's only then apparent, like fastidious fingers.
The line's familiar; I've seen it too
in thin fritillary leaves, in the flexed wings
of hawking martins and in the tapered paws
of cats cleaning the small circle of
their whiskered jowls. The link is strange
but obvious — perhaps if I were philosopher
enough I'd understand the natural ratio that
it illustrates in all these things but most
in limes, the tree I've chosen to outlive me.

Generations

No children see their parents in their prime
(the getting them was spice of that bright time);

so when another sixteen years have passed
and children turn enquiring eyes at last

upon familiar faces of their youth
they only see the middle-ageing truth.

They'll never know how long hair suited me,
how blond you were, how we walked amorously

down evening lanes in Somerset and Kent
(do they think hawthorn thickets were just meant

for present youth's philandering alone?)
Come now, they in their turn will moan

time's revolution, seeing their children's eyes
widen with that same disquieting surprise.

Button Oak To Arley

You would not think, on this quiet woodland track,
drama would be so near; but turn and take
the eastward lane that passes round the back
of that blue-painted cottage by the oak.
It keeps quite level for perhaps half a mile
then drops abruptly, its descent concealed
by its precipitation, alpine style,
between high hedge-bank, thorn, and barley field,

and comes on narrow meadows suddenly,
a wide fast stream, and wooded hills each side,
air thick with slanting birds, martin and swift,

— the River Severn shouldering steadily,
above the reach here of the highest tide,
secret and sensual in its oak-furred rift.

No Visionary Vegetable

This is no visionary vegetable like the Shoreham
apple trees, lifts no rose bosom to the clouds,
is not aureoled with pink; its disposition's
angular so that its branches spike the sky
and flowers only tuft the twigs, as is the way
of lesser trees.
                              But when this poorer show
is done it bears a crop magnificent as those
of the Hesperides, apples sulphur-green then glimmering
as legends, bowing the branches to the autumn earth
so that this narrow profile's rounded by fecundity
— a characteristic common to us both.

Race Memory

A dog in the distance barking
on wet nights transubstantiates
suburbia, turns lamp posts into trees,
iron entrances to wooden gates,
puts out the lights.
                              Across black valleys
from a vanished farm he barks
and in the gutters freeze small animals
and foxes prick their ears in parks.

Certain Things Envied

The children I knew in Wiltshire
when I was a child
were only one generation removed
from countrymen. There were still
grandparents farming beyond Faringdon,
aunts and uncles with long
bright gardens in the downs.
So their whole world of back-to backs,
small yards that lodged the mangle
and the new kittens, the morning hooter,
was irradiated by
the golden certainty of country holidays.

Come August and the pale town children
went to live a life I could only
imagine, enviously; they had
shrubberies, lofts, huge rhubarb plantations,
barns long disused to explore,
plum harvests to gather. They acquired
gold thatches to their brown town-heads.
Every day they climbed on those
pure-profiled hills and came back, hungrily,
to ham and lardy-cake for tea.
Each night settled them to sleep
in low rooms cosy with ceiling.
And every morning for
that one long glorious month
the satin scrape of wings against the eaves
half-woke them in the white
of dawn when the swallows woke.

Severn Harvests

i

They're thrifty around Severn; where the fields
slope, red and shining, to the west or south,
they plant small damson trees along the banks
as extra safeguards against storm or drouth,

netting the wind, consolidating soil.
They also add new beauty to the lane,
advantage to the eye as well as hand;
should double harvest too — there's fruit and grain.

ii

The theory works. After an edge-flowered spring,
the red soil greens, in thin and tenuous lines
that strengthen, heighten, grow in bulk and gold,
until the corn, in summer fullness, shines,

Therefore the combine harvester moves in
that does the work with little aid from men
though must be steered and oiled and kept in trim.
So is the first crop cut, and baled. And then

iii

men put the long, light ladders up to pick
the last, September, harvest of the year
— the roadside damsons' clusters, cobalt-blue,
mysterious in their trees' now golden sere,

which are coaeval with the rusting hedge,
sharing its duties and a common root,
so that it's something of gratuity,
this economical and velvet fruit.

Piper's Hill

All summer
the lands from Piper's Hill
were solid shape, the hedges'
regularity joining massed sage
and prussian blue where distance
misted the woods of Warwickshire.
Now colour separates and age
makes individuals of them all, edges
the tags of forest with rusting oaks
that stain towards the darker heart
of evergreen on higher contour lines,
yellows a stand of elms, pokes
a fiery finger on an outcast beech
beyond the cricket field. Apart
they stand, their distances revealed,
six yards or half a mile.
Acres obtrude.
Field paths link braided coverts,
ash and cinnamon, solitude
nobles a copse that now seems
Broceliande and lanes
of surprising sulphur twist away
among what seemed an undivided wood.

All autumn
I enjoy these distanced colours without shame
for nothing's moribund;
next year's recession too will set
match to this identifying flame.

Wyre Forest

This upland's quiet, with little sound of men
and small variety of plant and bird.
Conifers are silencing the native woods,
ousting the oaks, and what is mostly heard
is what a Dorset man remarked — the sigh
of wind in supple twigs of evergreen
as soon as they are set.

                        The elements
inhabit this high land, this flat-washed scene
of forest, heather, distances; the airs
of every month here carry scents of spruce,
rain wipes the narrow leaves; sun encourages
the saplings' growth so fast it hardly spares
the last small fields. Now, any man would choose
a lowland farm, with sweet deciduous hedges.

E

A Small Observance

Corruption is abroad.

I smell
the scent that warned my ancestors
that hawthorn flowers were on the verge
of tarnishing. This blossom festers
as does human flesh (the same change,
chemically, takes place, they say)
and so, because it smelt of death,
men did not bring indoors the may.

We are too wise these days to think
such correspondence means a thing,
to credit superstition or
recall these crowned the year's doomed king.
But still I do not like this scent.
I put the jug with sprigs of may
the children picked outside the kitchen door.
I will not court decay.

Revelation

The wood was fenced and barbed, preserved
for its own sake alone or because
woodland is not taxed
so hard. Certainly nothing of use
grew there; and we had never seen
its depths, it being a prehistoric wood
of small oaks, dwarf birches, brambles
almost as tall as trees — in summer
thick with leaves, in winter dark.

One January day though, tiring
of the house, we drove that way
and came on that fenced road
between the trees, expecting nothing but
the usual gloom. The snow
was thawing but its rags not yet
entirely gone. They strewed the verges,
a crisp and foreign substance, quite
different from the grey grass underneath.
They also lay in hollows of the wood.

I turned my head, without enthusiasm,
and suddenly saw the thin
white definition of the place —
its shape, extent, contours of hillocks,
ridges, only yards from the road,
that I'd not seen in greener
or browner times. Only the shrinking snow
revealed all this and, likely,
such a state of thaw and I
would not coincide again.

These Shropshire marches carry his name
for those who know him well although
he was no native of these parts. Shropshire
for him was the sight and then the memory
of blue-ridged hills in the West, on the horizon,
seen from the field above his home
in Worcestershire; but his own particular
equivocal nostalgia lurks about these lanes
and blends most easily with what must always be
an element of difference for Englishmen who
travel the other side of Severn.

                        How his thinking
still pervades this countryside! Unexpectedly
one afternoon, exploring high land not quite
hills north-east of Ludlow, we came upon
a village football match. A grey sky pressed
from Wenlock Edge to Bredon, goal posts
stood white against the mulberry hedge,
the pitch was summertime's rough grazing, just
the size. Boys with intent and rosy faces
and jerseys bright as paint dodged in the mud;
the lane was packed with unexpected cars
and men leaned shouting upon gateposts,
roofs, and bonnets, loud and uninhibited.
We did not stop, for all the gaiety — we were
so patently outsiders — but had to slow to pass
and saw it all in one quick eager stare.

Now, what was there about that scene to
set the mind upon mortality, and unrequited love,
and distances of man from man? Only his images,
his words, echoing in the memory to make
a microcosm of a mucky country game.

Seminal Image

The Vale first took my sight of course
as we came over the hill like that
athwart the sunset thirty years ago.
A cobalt width and depth of distances
seemed to extend my sight in width and depth;
elms furred and striped the meadows lit
by the last slanting light and Cotswold lay beyond,
the lighter blue of higher land.

                    I saw that first;
but, before we plunged into the valley's darker roads,
I glanced aside and was amazed
by hills on either hand, upon my level,
facing sunset full and brazenly, the miles of grass
like brass, like gold. Every hollow, track,
each tussock almost, thorns and junipers,
rabbit holes, chalkpits, old fortifications,
exposed themselves in detail, extending
bare and bright to evening light
and my astonished gaze.

                    Such a sight
still moves me most, for various reasons
I do not define — landscape in last light,
viridian, bronze, and vulnerable, facing
and participating in the death of day.

A Late Spring

To one familiar with the shadows
of the wood it's odd to see them
thin as this at this sweet time of year
as they grow shorter past the equinox.
Mid-April should deposit them
thickening with almost-broken buds
upon the floor of last year's leaves.

Clear sky, strong sun, but a north wind,
so the season's late. One small
strange thing makes up for lack
of vernal leaves — a sense
of wide attentiveness among the trees,
along the hedgerows, which is not
at first explicable. But then
it dawns on me I do not often see
the sun reflect so whitely back
from such a height and I am witnessing
the bare bright stare of leafless branches
like unlidded eyes, shining and sinister.

I Question A Victory

These are the days that penetrate my defences
when grasses on verges flower in sunlight,
when ferns are young and green to walk among,
when books and poetry are no protection from
memories of breakers I'll never see again or
the sounds of voices in nearby sunny gardens
and feet ringing on the pavements beyond the hedge.

Unlike Thomas Grey whom sunshiny weather
could always cure of melancholy I know that
brighter days do not make this situation better,
nor holidays; the contrast is too pointed.
But who, after all, is more glad than I that the grasses
and ferns will repeat themselves in self-sufficiency
for many years, sunlit, oblivious of men?

Not The Dead Of Winter

Not the dead of winter but the dying, late
November in fact and the trees quite bare
in the wood as we come, its condition
damp, its floor felted with leaves; and yet I swear
I smell violets, sweet in that biting air.

A foolish notion. All frost and snow are yet to come,
four months till spring and any expectation
of flowers among the trunks — and yet I smell
violets, so strong I look to see their station
beneath the hazels, their blue illumination.

London streets smelt like that when I was first
in love! Now it is nearly twenty years
and love's more sober. Not that, then. Just delight
perhaps so to be out-of-doors? Weekday fears
are soon dispelled as Saturday's reprieve appears.

I sit and sniff, knowing I'm mistaken,
but woodland smells are good, whatever season.
Soon we must go home, I know. I will not say
I have smelt violets without any reason.
We'll find them open in their proper season.

The Gaze

The room in which I sit all day
is crook'd like an elbow to the house itself
so that I look across the garden but also up
at the windows and they reflect the western skies
and — most magnificently — the north-west clouds
that come downwind in autumn. So I get
double pleasure from this place, the sight
of what's to come and then the sight
of their procession going down the miles of sky,
over the oak, the ash, the spire, the hidden road
in the valley, the rest of the unseen shire.

Sometimes though a cloud comes up like this
— cumulus castellatus — and I do not chance
to be looking up, I am writing, or reading.
I feel it though as one feels a person's
gaze. I look up. It is invisible to me
in its reality as yet but bears down
in that width of dark reflecting glass
— white, gold-edged, most powerful —
looking upon me as a ghost might look,
intent from the window, perhaps
not malevolent, but penetrating.

After The Apotheosis

The lovely music dies. The rose-pink
    satin's laid aside.
They are left alone in the gardens,
    the prince and his bride.

Beyond the walls where nettles
    breed butterflies
the talking fox that helped them
    silently lifts gold eyes;

the leather, inexhaustible,
    thonged bag is thrust
into a disused store-room
    to conceive, now, only dust;

the man who could drink rivers
    tosses back a beer,
hitches his trousers and ambles
    into Parchedshire.

They did their duty, followed
    the story's track.
Now the magic's over. Earth, attic,
    meadow, take them back.

Cley Eye (1968)

Geographically speaking, this
bank of shingle's significant,
mounting, eroded, mounting
again over the centuries, creating
marshes behind it and cutting
the village off from the sea.

This morning the wind's north-west.
The breakers are hurled on the bank
and hiss back like an indrawn
breath, straining between the stones.
Clouds like the crests of combers
sail in on the same blue tide.

This is my last view of the sea
or rather, my last hearing. Wheels
will not surmount that bank so
I sit in the marshes and listen,
knowing the geography but only
remembering the movement.

A bitter moment with a sort
of grin to it — I might as well
have stayed at home. I cannot make
another journey to the English coast. If
I'd looked at the map with more attention
I might have foreseen this irony.

The Track To The Beach

The track to the beach was through
a wood — of thorn perhaps or tamarisk,
certainly tall enough to be dark.
The meadows this side were bright
and the sands beyond sunlit. Three years old,
I tagged along at the back and saw people
going down narrow paths, calling
to each other, laughing, in brilliant blue
and orange and striped pink
among the shadows. There were
butterflies seemingly tangled in the
thin branches; these were all blue.

When I read Dante first, many years later,
I saw quite clearly again the procession
of bright damned souls in the dark wood.

Religion Of Some Use

Something startled the jackdaws. I watch them rise
and clank in the grey afternoon and hurl themselves
into the currents round St. John's fine spire,
undulating restlessly before the shelves

of stonework, gargoyles, finials, part play,
part true alarm. Ambivalence makes them vocal.
This noisy dancing is on private winds
whose origins are far but variations local.

Masons and steeplejacks have sometimes felt these airs
but finally it is the jackdaws' world alone,
spiralling on turbulence outside their platformed nests
built in the echoing apex of brown stone.

Men made that world however. Had they not built that spire,
planted those limes, the view for me would be aimless
and, the wind unfractured in its headlong course,
the jackdaws not only homeless but gameless.

Upstairs Light

That particular light begins about half-way
upstairs — a brighter daylight than in kitchen,
hall, or living room, less overshadowed and reduced
by neighbours' walls or lilacs given their heads.
It sparkles. It floods the upper stair-well,
the austere landing, bleaches the bedspreads,
slides along walls, glares from the bathroom tiles.
I, at ground level now, remember it longingly.

Philosophically speaking, of course, it still exists
although, because I do not see it now, it seems
a thing of the past; I used to see, from upstairs windows,
the crystal bases of clouds, the sunset, the lupins
next-door-but-two, the winter stars. It lit
the morning ritual of making beds, of making up.
It spiced afternoon love-making. It illumined
the heads of children asleep.

It was a brighter world, upstairs.

Holidays, Explorations

How can I bear it that
journeying's over
while still the heart's un-
regenerate rover,

still longs to visit
strange hamlet, strange river,
to feel at view's width
the authentic shiver?

Now I must practise
good grace at parting,
to wish others joy though
I am not starting

the ride through the sunrise
to valleys of vision.
I fix on my smile now
with summer precision.

After The Requested Cremation

A steady north-north-west wind preferably,
though an east wind would do as second-best,
and so my bones' smoke and innocent ashes
would carry into Wessex or the west.

I'd like my dust to be deposited
in the dry ditches, among the fine grass of home,
on hills I've walked, in furrows I've watched making
in Wiltshire's chalk-bright loam.

If not that then Wolverhampton's chimneys
might send me Severnward; that would do instead.
Those rose-red farms, those orchards, have all been
                                precious.
I'd like to fertilize them when I'm dead.

Make no mistake though, it'll not come to choosing.
There'll be a west wind in the week I go.
Or else my southern dust will fall on hated highways
and be for ever swirling to and fro.

Well, as I'll never know, it doesn't matter.
I'm not, in truth, romantic about death.
Only I'd like the right wind to be blowing
that takes the place of breath.

60703

HOLDEN, MOLLY
    ATR AND CHILL EARTH.

DATE DUE

GAYLORD   PRINTED IN U.S.A.